Eid

This book belongs to

____

PEGASUS

www.pegasusforkids.com

Published by Kuldeep Jain for B. Jain Publishers (P) Ltd., D-157, Sector 63, Noida - 201307, U.P

Printed in India

This graded series is written in easy-to-understand English. The aim is to develop reading habit in children and to increase their vocabulary.

Eid al-Fitr is the Islamic festival of breaking the fast and Eid-al-Adha is the Islamic festival of sacrifice.

Eid al-Fitr is celebrated at the end of the holy month of Ramadan. During Ramadan, Muslims fast from dawn to dusk.

Ramadan is said to be the month when Prophet Muhammad was first visited by the angel Jibral.

Jibral carried God's word and this was written down by Prophet Muhammad in the form of the holy Quran.

Eid al-Fitr is celebrated to mark the end of the month-long fasting.

Eid al-Fitr begins when the first sight of the new moon is seen in the sky.

On Eid al-Fitr, Muslims offer special prayers in mosques and break the fast with a sweet dish.

On Eid al-Adah, a cattle animal is sacrificed to mark Ibrahim's willingness to sacrifice his son for God.

The meat is then divided into three parts: one for the family, one for friends and relatives, and one for the poor. Special prayer is offered in mosques.

Families and friends gather together to exchange gifts and eat traditional food.

Everyone wears new clothes and offer best wishes to each other.

Older members of the family also give money to children on Eid al-Adha. This is called Eidi.

Eid is also a time for people to donate to the poor and to those in need.

Both the Eids are celebrated with great gusto throughout the world by Muslims.

New words to learn

fast	prophet
sacrifice	celebrated
dawn	prayers
dusk	special
cattle	willingness
exchange	gusto